the HUMAN BODY activity book FOR KIDS

the HUMAN BODY activity book FOR KIDS

HANDS-ON FUN FOR GRADES K-3

KATIE STOKES, M.Ed., Ph.D.

Illustrations by Christy Ni

ROCKRIDGE PRESS

To my mom: Thank you for sparking my interest in science.

To my husband: Your never-ending support means the world to me.
Thank you for backing my crazy ideas and encouraging me to shine.

To my children: You inspire me to be more creative,
more fun, and more loving. You are the reason I do what I do.

Interior Designer: Katy Brown
Cover Designer: Kristine Brogno
Editor: Katharine Moore
Production Editor: Erum Khan
Illustrations © Christy Ni

ISBN: Print 978-1-64152-263-2

CONTENTS

LETTER TO PARENTS AND TEACHERS

Dear Parents and Teachers,

I'm honored that you have selected this activity book to help your children and students learn about the human body.

I have written this book to empower them with important knowledge about how their bodies work. Most children are naturally curious about their bodies, and by capitalizing on their fascination we lay the foundation for them to experience greater health and enjoyment throughout their lives.

My passion for science education started when I was young. My mom was a middle school science teacher and she passed her love of science on to me. It was because of her that I decided to study human biology as a college undergraduate. Today, I combine my science background with my knowledge of child development to create engaging science materials I share with parents and teachers on my blog, *Gift of Curiosity*.

Over the years, having a degree in human biology has served my family and me well. Because I understand the human body, I am able to communicate competently with our health care providers, and I am well positioned to make choices that keep my family healthy and strong. My hope is that this book is an early step that will allow your child to be similarly empowered as they grow.

Each section of this book reviews a different body system. I have included information about the role and importance of each system, a detailed visual diagram, and fun facts about the system. Children learn best when they are having fun, so every section includes an activity designed to maximize engagement and further the learning process. The main activities in each section can all be done right in the book with a pencil and crayons or markers.

As part of each section, there is a suggested activity your child can do at home to continue exploring the specific body system. Your support to help your child complete the at-home activities will be invaluable.

This book is intended for early elementary students in kindergarten through third grade. Children on the younger end of this range will need your help working through the book, while older children can do more on their own.

As a parent and educator, I believe we serve our children best when we follow their lead. As such, I invite you to allow your child to work through the sections in this book in whatever order they wish.

It is my sincere hope that the information and activities in this book will spark your child's interest in learning more about the human body. Please see the back of the book for additional resources your child can use to continue learning about their amazing body.

—Katie Stokes, ME.d., Ph.D.
FOUNDER OF *GIFT OF CURIOSITY*

ALL ABOUT
YOUR BODY

Bodies come in all shapes, sizes, and colors. Your body may be tall or short, thick or thin, light-skinned or dark-skinned. Your body is changing and growing all the time. But even though bodies look different, they all do similar things. Your body helps you see, hear, smell, taste, and touch. It helps you run, climb, talk, and learn. Celebrate your body for all it helps you do!

A person can lose their stomach, spleen, one kidney, one lung, most of their liver, and most of their intestines and still survive. However, they wouldn't be very healthy.

The average American man is 5 feet 9 inches tall and weighs 196 pounds. The average American woman is 5 feet 3 inches tall and weighs 169 pounds.

TOP 5 FUN FACTS

1. You grow faster in the spring than during any other season.

2. You are taller in the morning than at night. This is because the padding between your bones, called *cartilage*, gets squeezed during the day, so you shrink. Overnight, the cartilage goes back to normal, so you are slightly taller when you wake up.

3. You will spend about 5 years of your life eating.

4. You will spend about 25 years of your life sleeping.

5. During your life, you will walk about 100,000 miles. This is like walking around the earth four times.

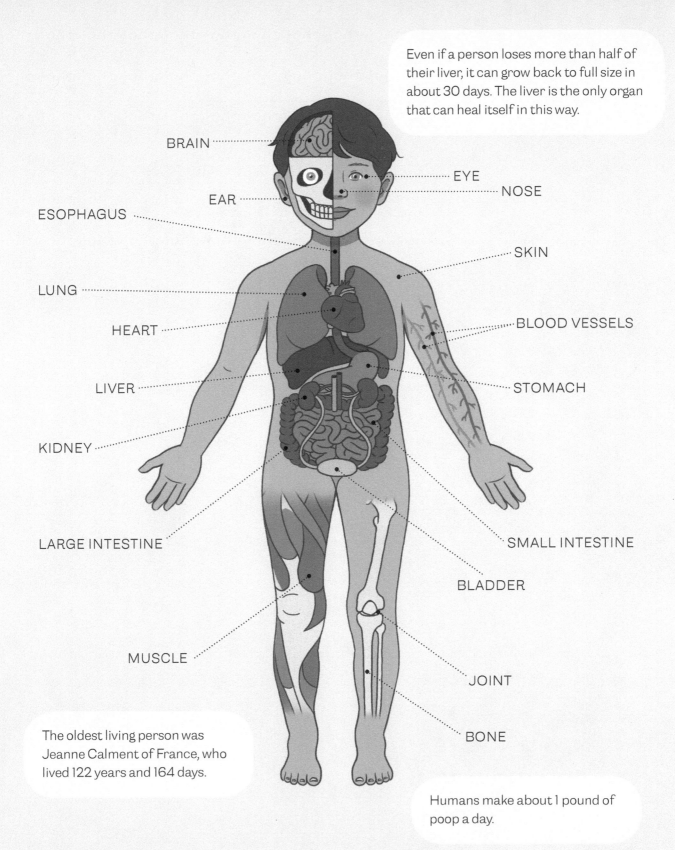

Even if a person loses more than half of their liver, it can grow back to full size in about 30 days. The liver is the only organ that can heal itself in this way.

BRAIN

EYE

NOSE

EAR

ESOPHAGUS

SKIN

LUNG

HEART

BLOOD VESSELS

LIVER

STOMACH

KIDNEY

SMALL INTESTINE

LARGE INTESTINE

BLADDER

MUSCLE

JOINT

BONE

The oldest living person was Jeanne Calment of France, who lived 122 years and 164 days.

Humans make about 1 pound of poop a day.

ALL ABOUT YOUR BODY

ACTIVITY

Fill in the blanks using the words in the word bank at the bottom of the page.

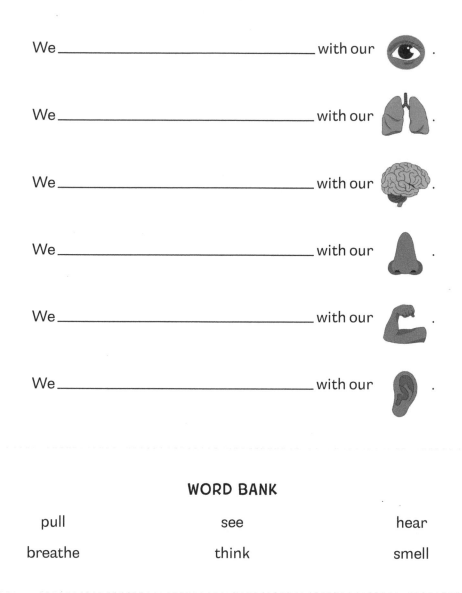

We _____ with our 👁 .

We _____ with our 🫁 .

We _____ with our 🧠 .

We _____ with our 👃 .

We _____ with our 💪 .

We _____ with our 👂 .

WORD BANK

pull	see	hear
breathe	think	smell

Without your body, life would be very different. Make a list of 10 (or more!) things your body allows you to do.

_____

_____

_____

_____

_____

_____

_____

_____

TEENY TINY: YOUR CELLS

Your body is made of trillions of tiny building blocks called *cells*. Each cell is like a little factory that does different jobs to help the body. Groups of cells join together to make bones, muscles, lungs, and other body parts that help you move, breathe, eat, and play. Keeping your cells healthy helps keep your whole body healthy.

Most cells are so small that they can only be seen with a microscope.

Cells were discovered in 1665 by a scientist named Robert Hooke.

Groups of similar cells join together to make organs and other important body parts.

TOP 5 FUN FACTS

1. Your body is made of almost 35 trillion cells. This means there are 5,000 times more cells in your body than there are people on earth.

2. The longest cells in the human body are motor neuron cells, which can grow to 4 ½ feet long in order to stretch from the brain to the muscles. However, these cells are so thin that they can only be seen under a microscope.

3. By the time you finish reading this sentence, 50,000 cells in your body will die and new cells will take their place.

4. New cells are made through a process called *mitosis*. During mitosis, a cell splits in half to make two identical new cells.

5. Bacteria are tiny living things. There are 10 times more bacteria cells than human cells in your body.

There are about 200 different kinds of cells in the human body, and they all have different jobs like carrying oxygen, protecting the body from germs, and helping you think.

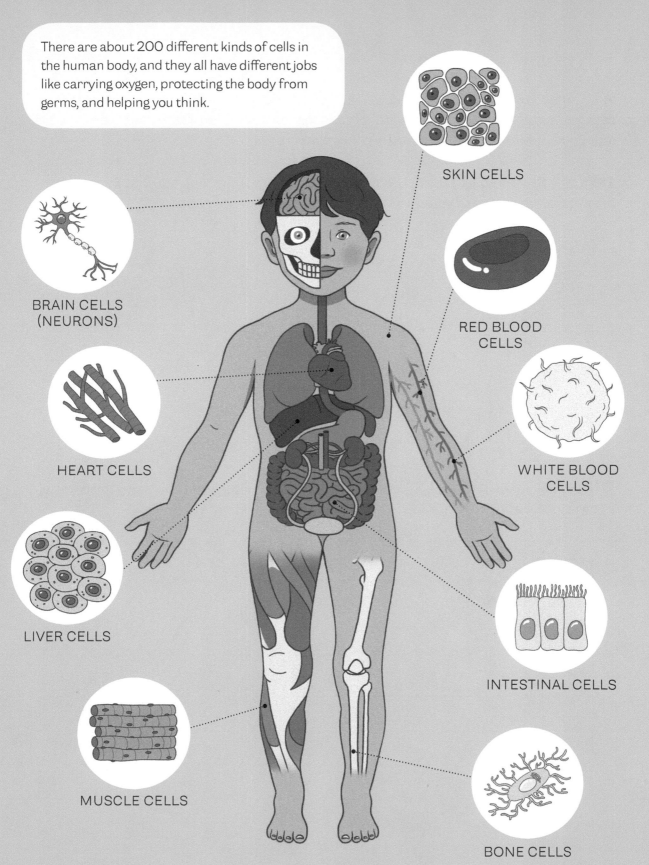

SKIN CELLS

BRAIN CELLS (NEURONS)

RED BLOOD CELLS

HEART CELLS

WHITE BLOOD CELLS

LIVER CELLS

INTESTINAL CELLS

MUSCLE CELLS

BONE CELLS

ACTIVITY

Your body is made of trillions of cells. This activity will help you understand how these cells work together. Draw pictures of organs that are made up of different types of cells. If needed, refer to the illustration on the previous page.

THIS IS A BRAIN CELL OR NEURON. Lots of brain cells work together to form your brain. Draw a picture of your brain.

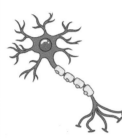

THESE ARE MUSCLE CELLS. Lots of muscle cells work together to form your muscles. Draw a picture of your muscles.

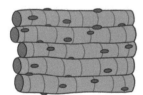

THESE ARE HEART CELLS. Lots of heart cells work together to form your heart. Draw a picture of your heart.

THIS IS A BONE CELL. Lots of bone cells work together to form your bones. Draw a picture of your bones.

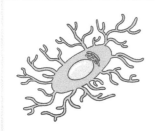

➡ **Try This at Home**

Ask an adult to help you use the Internet or go to your library to find a picture of a cell and its parts. Then use materials you have at home to build a model of a cell. Get creative! For example, you can build a cell out of food, toys, or craft supplies.

BARE BONES: YOUR SKELETON

Bones are strong, stiff organs that make up your skeleton. Your bones have many important jobs. One job is to give your body its shape. Without bones, your skin would fall to the ground! A second job of your bones is to work with your muscles to help you move. A third job is to protect the organs inside your body. A fourth job is to make blood cells and store minerals your body needs to stay healthy. As you can see, your bones do a lot more than just give you your shape!

TOP 5 FUN FACTS

1. A quarter of all the bones in your body are in your feet. One adult foot has 26 bones and 33 joints.

2. Inside your bones is a soft, spongy material called *bone marrow*. Your bone marrow makes new blood cells.

3. The longest bone in your body is the femur, or thigh bone.

4. The smallest bone in your body is the stapes bone, found inside your ear.

5. Your teeth are part of your skeletal system but are not counted as bones.

➡ **Try This at Home**

Make a model of the human skeleton by gluing pasta pieces or cotton swabs on black paper in the shape of your skeleton. You can use the skeleton picture on the next page or an image you find online to help you design your model.

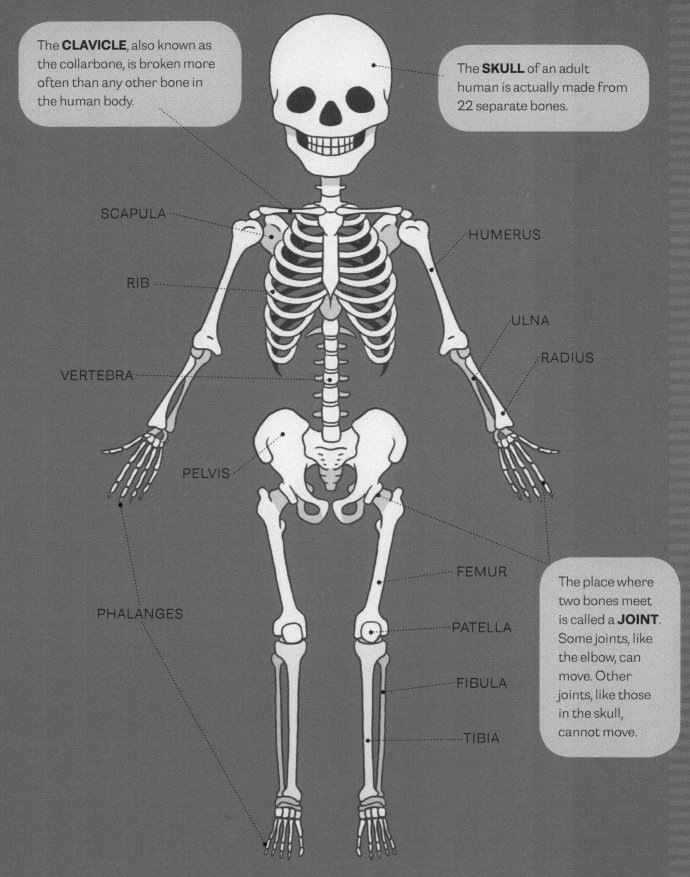

The **CLAVICLE**, also known as the collarbone, is broken more often than any other bone in the human body.

The **SKULL** of an adult human is actually made from 22 separate bones.

SCAPULA

HUMERUS

RIB

ULNA

RADIUS

VERTEBRA

PELVIS

PHALANGES

FEMUR

The place where two bones meet is called a **JOINT**. Some joints, like the elbow, can move. Other joints, like those in the skull, cannot move.

PATELLA

FIBULA

TIBIA

ACTIVITY

Color the **skull** bones yellow.

Color the **rib** and **vertebra** bones red.

Color the **phalanges** in the **fingers** and **toes** orange.

Color the **clavicle** and **scapula** bones in the shoulders gray.

Color the **humerus**, **radius**, and **ulna** bones in the arms green.

Color the **pelvis** blue.

Color the **femur**, **fibula**, and **tibia** bones in the legs purple.

Babies are born with about 300 bones, but as children grow, some of their bones grow together. Adults only have 206 bones.

Pound for pound, human bones are five times stronger than steel.

SUPER STRONG:
YOUR MUSCLES

You probably already know you have muscles that help your body move. We call the muscles that help with movement *skeletal* muscles. But did you know that you also have two other types of muscles? *Cardiac* muscles pump blood through your heart and body, and *smooth* muscles help you breathe, digest your food, and move blood through your body. While skeletal muscles rest a lot, cardiac and smooth muscles never rest. You can't control your cardiac muscles or smooth muscles. However, they do very important work in your body to keep you alive and healthy.

TOP 5 FUN FACTS

1. When you get stronger, you do not grow new muscle fibers. Instead, the fibers you already have get thicker.

2. If all of the skeletal muscles in your body could pull in one direction at the same time, they would create a force of 25 tons. That's enough strength to lift four elephants!

3. The largest muscle in your body is the one you sit on: your gluteus maximus.

4. The strongest muscle in your body (the one that can create the most pressure) is your *masseter*. This jaw muscle helps you chew your food.

5. Forty percent of your body weight is made up of muscle.

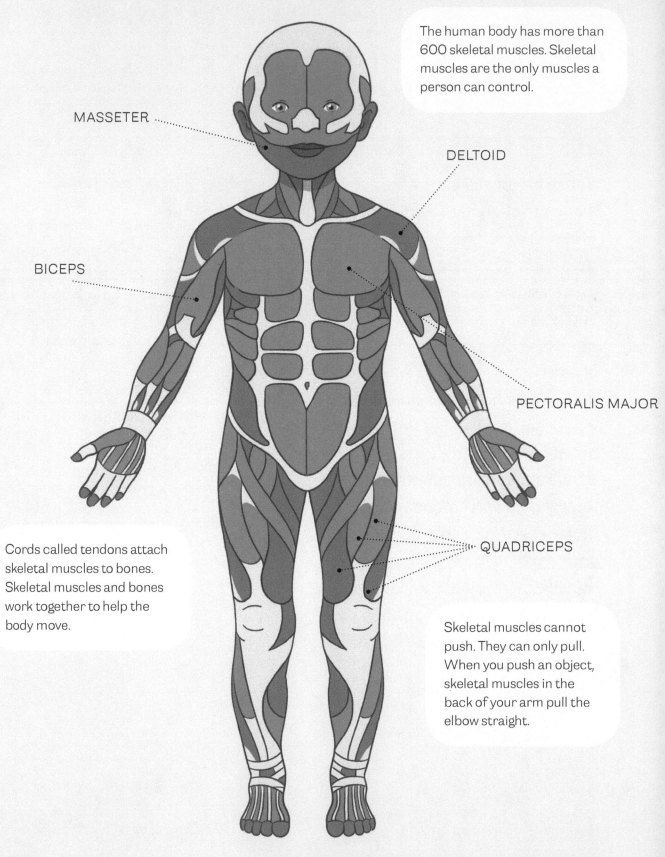

The human body has more than 600 skeletal muscles. Skeletal muscles are the only muscles a person can control.

MASSETER

DELTOID

BICEPS

PECTORALIS MAJOR

Cords called tendons attach skeletal muscles to bones. Skeletal muscles and bones work together to help the body move.

QUADRICEPS

Skeletal muscles cannot push. They can only pull. When you push an object, skeletal muscles in the back of your arm pull the elbow straight.

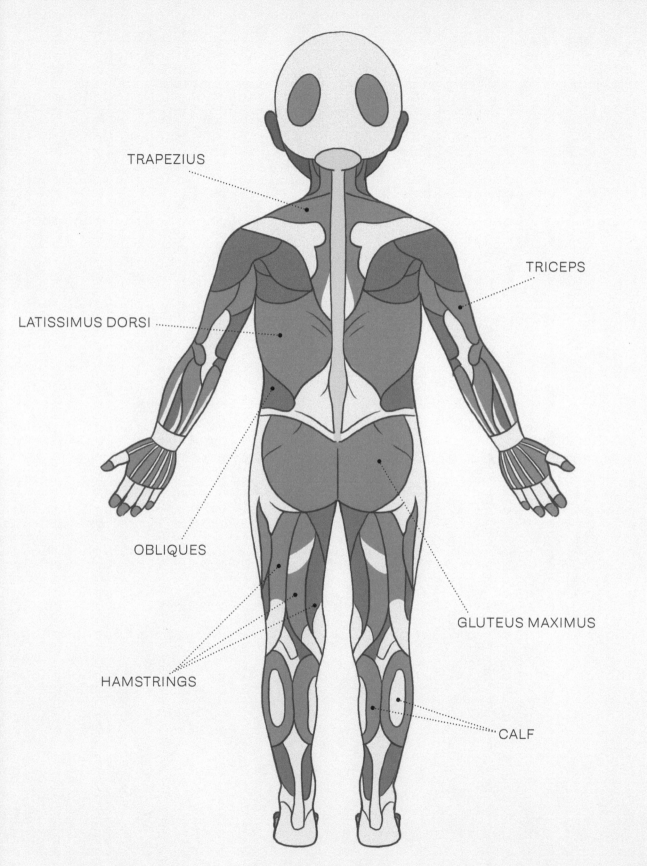

TRAPEZIUS

TRICEPS

LATISSIMUS DORSI

OBLIQUES

GLUTEUS MAXIMUS

HAMSTRINGS

CALF

ACTIVITY

Draw a picture of yourself doing an activity that uses the **masseter muscles** in your jaw.

Draw a picture of yourself doing an activity that uses the **biceps muscles** in your arms.

Draw a picture of yourself doing an activity that uses the **calf muscles** in your legs.

➡ **Try This at Home**

Ask an adult to help you use the Internet or take you to the library to find information about exercises you can do to strengthen your muscles. Try out at least one exercise that will strengthen the muscles in your arms and one exercise that will strengthen the muscles in your legs.

ON THE OUTSIDE:
YOUR SKIN, HAIR, AND NAILS

Your skin, your hair, your nails. Even though we often think about how these body parts *look*, we don't often think about what they *do*. But your skin, hair, and nails all have important jobs!

Your skin is your largest organ and it has several duties. It blocks germs from entering your body. It makes sweat to keep your body from getting too hot. It also allows you to touch and feel things.

Your hair keeps you warm and protects you. Your eyebrows, for example, keep sweat out of your eyes.

Your nails protect your fingertips from getting hurt. They help you do useful things, too. Without your fingernails, it would be hard to scratch an itch or untie a knot.

TOP 5 FUN FACTS

1. You get a new epidermis—top layer of skin—every 30 days. This means that your skin completely changes every month.

2. Your body grows hair everywhere except the palms of your hands, the soles of your feet, and your lips.

3. Your hair grows more slowly at night than in the daytime, and faster in summer than in winter.

4. Fingernails grow about four times faster than toenails.

5. Under your skin, the roots of your hair are alive. But the hair coming out of your skin is dead. That is why it doesn't hurt to get a haircut.

Every square inch of skin contains thousands of cells and hundreds of sweat glands, oil glands, nerve endings, and blood vessels.

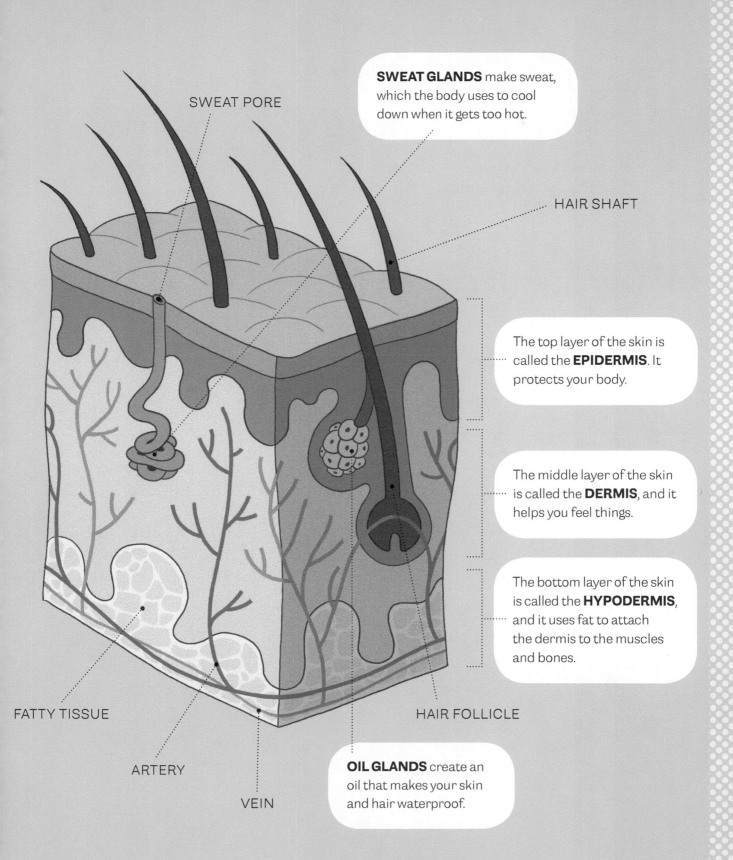

SWEAT PORE

SWEAT GLANDS make sweat, which the body uses to cool down when it gets too hot.

HAIR SHAFT

The top layer of the skin is called the **EPIDERMIS**. It protects your body.

The middle layer of the skin is called the **DERMIS**, and it helps you feel things.

The bottom layer of the skin is called the **HYPODERMIS**, and it uses fat to attach the dermis to the muscles and bones.

FATTY TISSUE

ARTERY

VEIN

HAIR FOLLICLE

OIL GLANDS create an oil that makes your skin and hair waterproof.

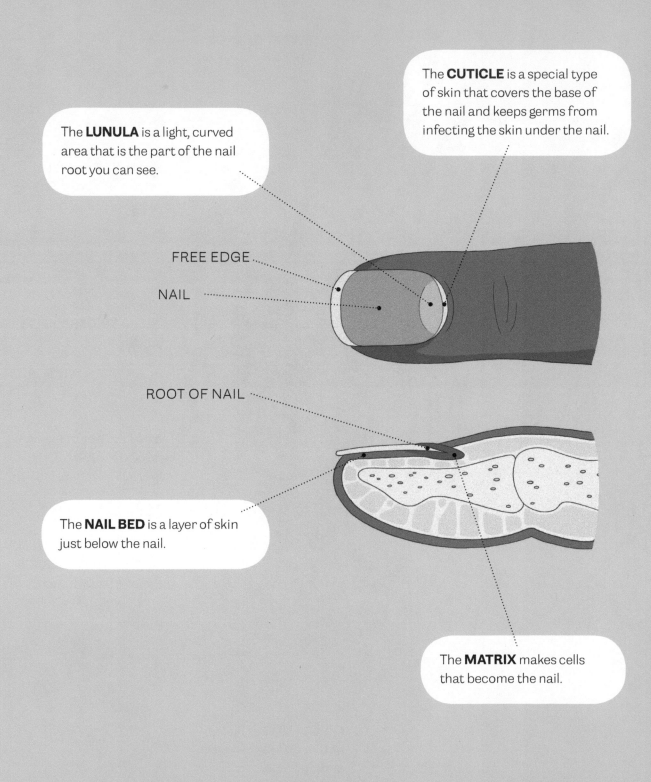

The **LUNULA** is a light, curved area that is the part of the nail root you can see.

The **CUTICLE** is a special type of skin that covers the base of the nail and keeps germs from infecting the skin under the nail.

FREE EDGE

NAIL

ROOT OF NAIL

The **NAIL BED** is a layer of skin just below the nail.

The **MATRIX** makes cells that become the nail.

ACTIVITY

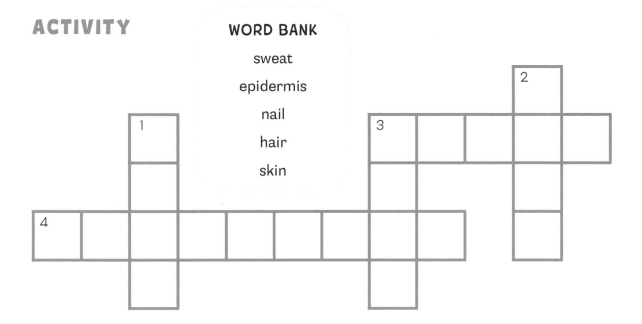

WORD BANK

sweat

epidermis

nail

hair

skin

Down

1. Keeps the top of your head warm
2. Helps you scratch an itch
3. Your body's largest organ, which stops germs from getting into your body

Across

3. Liquid your skin makes to keep you from getting too hot
4. The top layer of the skin

➡ Try This at Home

Have a partner gather several items and put each one into separate paper bags. Be sure the items don't have sharp edges or anything else that might hurt you.

Put on a blindfold. Then have your partner hand you one of the bags. Reach inside and feel the item. Using only your sense of touch, can you guess what the item is?

KNOW IT ALL:
YOUR BRAIN AND NERVOUS SYSTEM

Your brain is like a powerful computer that talks to every part of your body. It sends messages through your nervous system, including your spinal cord and nerves, to tell your body parts what to do. Nerves also send information from your eyes, ears, nose, mouth, and skin to tell your brain what is going on in your world.

TOP 5 FUN FACTS

1. Your brain is just 2 percent of your body weight. However, it uses around 20 percent of your energy, enough to power a night-light.

2. There are more nerve cells in your brain than there are stars in the galaxy.

3. Your brain sends more messages to your body each day than all the phones in the world. That's a lot of texting!

4. Information can travel along your nerves at speeds of up to 250 miles per hour. That's faster than most race cars!

5. Damage to the nervous system can make it impossible to move certain body parts, a condition known as paralysis.

The **CEREBRUM** makes up 85 percent of your brain's weight. It helps with thinking and muscle movements.

The **CEREBELLUM** controls balance and movement. It also helps your muscles work together.

The **BRAIN** has two halves. Nerves cross sides when they enter and leave the brain, so the left side of the brain controls the right half of the body and the right side of the brain controls the left half of the body.

The **BRAIN STEM** controls breathing, digestion, and the beating of your heart. It also connects to the spinal cord.

SPINAL CORD

NERVES

ACTIVITY

Help the signal travel through the brain to reach the body by tracing a line through the maze.

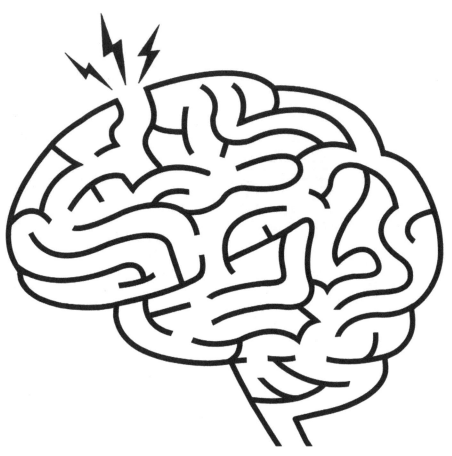

➡ Try This at Home

A *reflex* is when your body reacts to something without you having to think about it. Reflexes are part of the nervous system. With a partner, you can test your knee-jerk reflex.

Sit on a chair with your legs crossed so that the leg on top swings freely. Find the soft spot just below the kneecap. Have your partner use the side of their hand to lightly hit your leg in that soft spot. If your partner hits the right place, your leg will kick out.

OPEN YOUR EYES: HOW YOU SEE

Your eyes are like small cameras that take pictures of the world around you. Those pictures come in through the pupils—the tiny black dots in the middle of each of your eyes—and get sent along the optic nerve to the brain. Your brain then uses those pictures to help you see.

➡ Try This at Home

Put several small objects on a table. Now cover one eye with your hand. Reach out and touch the top of one object. It's hard to do with only one eye! Now open both eyes and try to touch the top of the object again. See how much easier that was?

Your brain needs information from both eyes to know how close or far away an object is. That's why it is easier to touch the object when both eyes are open.

TOP 5 FUN FACTS

1 When you were born, you could only see the colors black, white, and gray. Now you can see 10 million different shades of color.

2 Many boys, and a smaller number of girls, are color blind. This means they cannot tell the difference between colors such as red and green or blue and yellow.

3 The picture your eye sees on the back of the retina is actually upside down. Your brain flips the image right side up for you to see.

4 You blink more than 10,000 times a day. Blinking removes dirt and stops your eyes from drying out.

5 It is impossible to keep your eyes open when you sneeze.

The human eyeball is about the size of a ping-pong ball and weighs less than 10 pennies.

EYEBROWS keep sweat from dripping into the eyes. They also help communicate your thoughts and opinions to others.

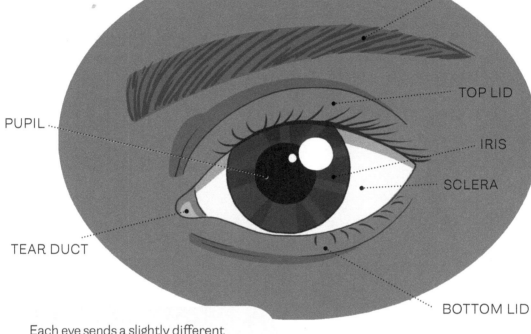

PUPIL

TEAR DUCT

TOP LID

IRIS

SCLERA

BOTTOM LID

Each eye sends a slightly different picture to the brain, and the brain uses that information to know how far away an object is.

Eye color comes from the amount of a material in the iris called *melanin*. The most common eye color is brown, followed by blue.

The **IRIS** is the colored part of the eye and the hole in the middle of the iris is the pupil. Muscles in the iris make the pupil bigger and smaller to change the amount of light going into the eye.

The **CORNEA** is a clear layer covering the front of the eye.

The **RETINA** is covered in small sensors that turn the picture the eyes see into an electrical signal that can be sent along the optic nerve to the brain.

PUPIL

The **LENS** changes shape to help the cornea focus light onto the retina.

OPTIC NERVE TO THE BRAIN

The **SCLERA** is a tough, white outer layer of the eyeball.

The **VITREOUS BODY** is a clear gel that fills the eyeball.

ACTIVITY

Your eyes take pictures of what is around you, and your brain uses the information from your eyes to help you see. But sometimes you can trick your brain into seeing things that aren't really there!

Make a Floating Finger Sausage

Hold your index fingers about 5 inches in front of your eyes, with the tips almost touching. Now look through your fingers and focus on something beyond them. Do you see the floating finger sausage? Try moving your hands in and out to see what happens.

Why do you see a floating "sausage" between your fingers? Even though your eyes are focused on something far away, they still see your fingers right in front of you. However, your eyes are only seeing part of your fingers. Your brain creates a "sausage" as it tries to make sense of the incomplete information it is getting.

The Magic Light Bulb

Stare closely at the light bulb picture for 15 seconds. Then immediately stare at a white wall or white sheet of paper. Do you see another light bulb appear?

Why do you see a glowing white light bulb? When you look at the black bulb for a long time, the cells on your retina get tired. When you look away, the cells that aren't tired react more strongly than the other cells, making what is called an "afterimage."

LEND AN EAR: HOW YOU HEAR

What can you hear right now? Someone talking? A bird chirping? A car engine running? If you can hear sounds, you should thank your ears! Your ears have three main parts—an outer ear, middle ear, and inner ear—that work to collect sounds from around you and send them to your brain.

TOP 5 FUN FACTS

1. Have you ever noticed that elderly people have big ears? The pinna of your outer ear never stops growing, so your ears keep getting bigger even after the rest of your body has reached full size.

2. Having two ears on opposite sides of your head allows you to figure out where a sound is coming from. Sounds enter one ear a little louder and sooner than the other ear, and your brain uses this information to figure out where the sound is coming from.

3. Your ears never stop hearing, even when you are asleep. However, your brain learns to ignore most sounds while you sleep so you can get a good night's rest.

4. Listening to very loud sounds, even for just a few minutes, can permanently hurt your hearing.

5. In addition to helping you hear, your ears help you stay balanced. Fluid in the inner ear tells your brain when your body is moving or tilted.

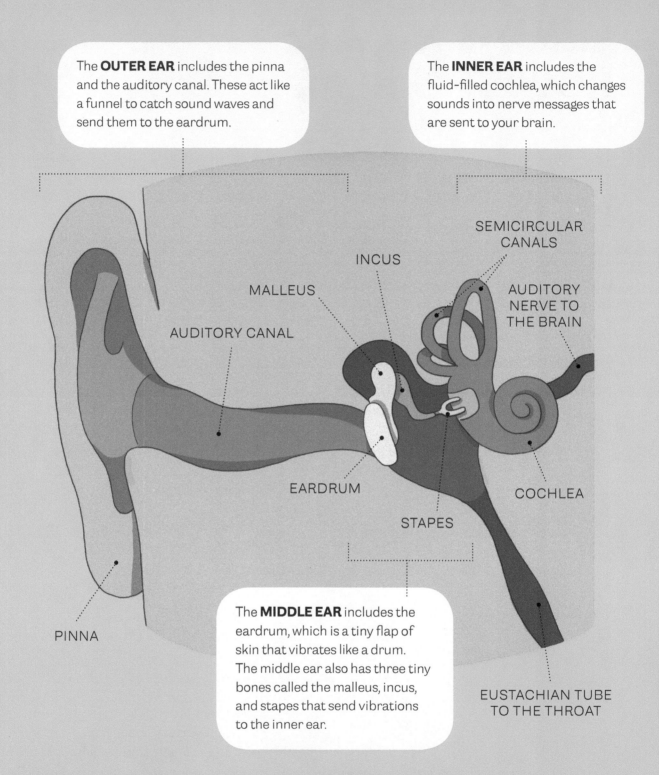

The **OUTER EAR** includes the pinna and the auditory canal. These act like a funnel to catch sound waves and send them to the eardrum.

The **INNER EAR** includes the fluid-filled cochlea, which changes sounds into nerve messages that are sent to your brain.

SEMICIRCULAR CANALS

INCUS

MALLEUS

AUDITORY NERVE TO THE BRAIN

AUDITORY CANAL

EARDRUM

COCHLEA

STAPES

PINNA

The **MIDDLE EAR** includes the eardrum, which is a tiny flap of skin that vibrates like a drum. The middle ear also has three tiny bones called the malleus, incus, and stapes that send vibrations to the inner ear.

EUSTACHIAN TUBE TO THE THROAT

ACTIVITY

Below, circle the things you can hear. Cross out the things you cannot hear.

➡ Try This at Home

Spin around 5 times really fast, then stop. Do you feel dizzy? Right after you stopped, the fluid in your ears kept spinning, telling your brain that you were moving, while your eyes told your brain that you were standing still. This confuses the brain and makes you feel dizzy.

THE NOSE KNOWS:
HOW YOU SMELL

Chocolate chip cookies. A ripe apple. Can you imagine the smell of these foods? If so, you have your nose to thank! Your nose helps you smell things. It also helps you breathe. Your nose filters and warms the air you breathe, sending air to your lungs and smells to your brain.

TOP 5 FUN FACTS

1. Your nose can smell more than one trillion different odors.

2. Your sense of smell helps keep you safe. For example, your nose tells you if food has gone bad and could make you sick, or if your home is on fire and you need to get out.

3. Some people with very sensitive noses get paid to sniff out smells in wines, perfumes, and factories.

4. You can smell another person's feelings, like fear, in their sweat.

5. Because of injury, illness, or age, some people lose their sense of smell. This is called *anosmia*.

➡ Try This at Home

Your sense of smell affects the taste of food. Take a bite of food. How does it taste? Now pinch your nose shut and take another bite. How does the taste of food change when you can't smell it?

The food likely lost some taste when you pinched your nose shut. This is because your sense of smell helps you taste your food better. When you can't smell, your food doesn't taste as good.

THE HUMAN BODY ACTIVITY BOOK FOR KIDS

Your **NOSTRILS** bring in air filled with tiny smell molecules.

NASAL
CAVITY

The smells reach the **OLFACTORY BULB**, which sends smell information to the brain.

When you smell something, your **BRAIN** reminds you about the people, places, things, and events related to the smell.

THE NOSE KNOWS: HOW YOU SMELL

ACTIVITY

The girl smells something nice. Draw it in the space below.

The boy smells something gross. Draw it in the space below.

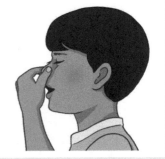

TIP OF YOUR TONGUE:
HOW YOU TASTE

A ripe strawberry. Homemade bread. We all have our favorite foods. But what makes a food taste good? Your tongue, of course! Your tongue is covered in tiny taste buds. When your saliva breaks down food, your taste buds sense whether the food is sweet, sour, salty, bitter, or savory. Your taste buds then send that information to your brain, and your brain tells you what flavors you are tasting.

TOP 5 FUN FACTS

1. You were born with about 10,000 taste buds in your mouth.

2. By the time you turn 60 years old, you will have lost half of your taste buds.

3. Girls have more taste buds than boys.

4. Your body can sense the taste of something faster than an eye can blink.

5. You cannot taste something until your saliva breaks it down.

➡ Try This at Home

In order for your tongue to taste something, your saliva has to dissolve it first. Put a sweet or salty food on your tongue. Notice how it tastes. Then use a towel to dry off your tongue. Put the same food on your tongue again. How does it taste now?

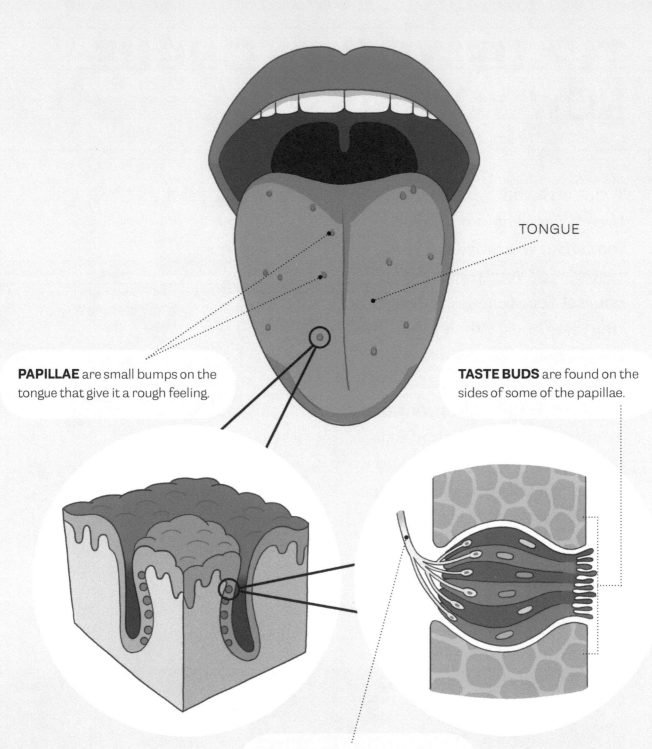

TONGUE

PAPILLAE are small bumps on the tongue that give it a rough feeling.

TASTE BUDS are found on the sides of some of the papillae.

The **SENSORY NERVE** carries flavor information from the taste buds to the brain.

THE HUMAN BODY ACTIVITY BOOK FOR KIDS

ACTIVITY

Connect the dots to find out what this girl's tongue is tasting.

Your tongue can taste sweet, salty, sour, bitter, and savory flavors. Circle your favorite flavor below.

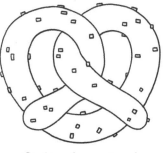

Salted pretzel

Sour lemon

Sweet candy

Bitter coffee

Savory mushroom

THE HUMAN BODY ACTIVITY BOOK FOR KIDS

TOUCHY FEELY:
HOW YOU FEEL

Your skin is the main organ that helps you feel things. When you touch something, special nerves in your skin called *sensory receptors* tell your brain whether the thing you are touching is rough, smooth, hot, or cold. Your skin receptors also tell you how hard you are pushing on an object and if the object is causing you pain. Information from your receptors travels along special sensory nerves to your brain.

TOP 5 FUN FACTS

1. Your fingers, toes, mouth, and lips are the most sensitive parts of the body because they have the most touch receptors.

2. The least sensitive part of your body is the middle of your back, as it has few touch receptors.

3. Your fingerprints make your sense of touch better by carrying touch signals to your nerves. They also ignore unimportant sensory information.

4. Your sense of touch gets worse as you get older.

5. When you scratch an itch, it creates a slight feeling of pain in your brain that competes with the itchy feeling in your brain. Your body prefers the pain of a scratch to the itchy feeling, so you feel better.

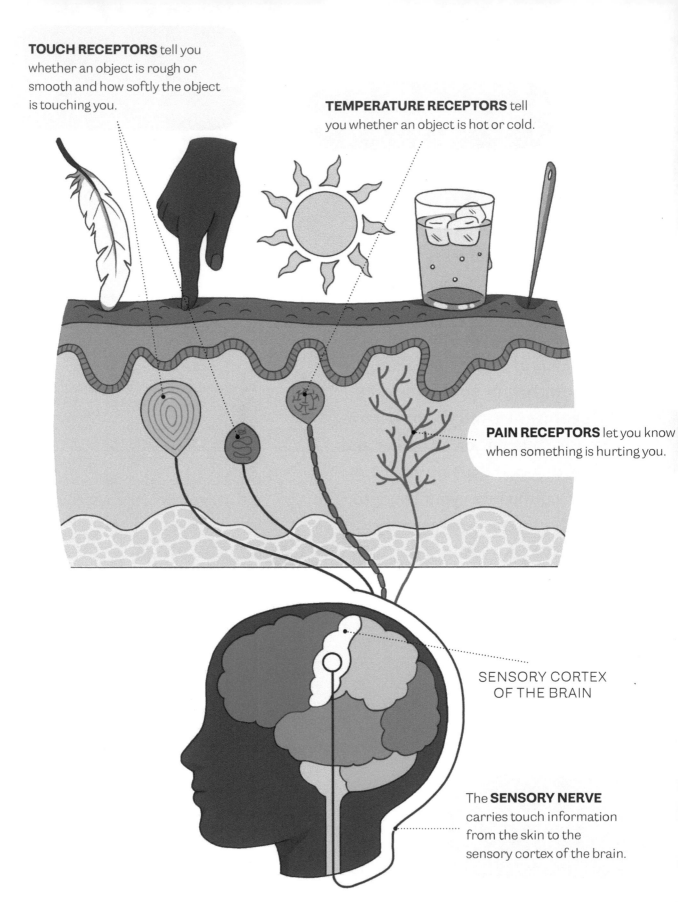

TOUCH RECEPTORS tell you whether an object is rough or smooth and how softly the object is touching you.

TEMPERATURE RECEPTORS tell you whether an object is hot or cold.

PAIN RECEPTORS let you know when something is hurting you.

SENSORY CORTEX OF THE BRAIN

The **SENSORY NERVE** carries touch information from the skin to the sensory cortex of the brain.

ACTIVITY

Draw a picture of something you touch at the beach. How does this thing feel?

Draw a picture of something you touch at home. How does this thing feel?

Draw a picture of something you touch at the park. How does this thing feel?

Draw a picture of something you touch at a restaurant. How does this thing feel?

➡ Try This at Home

Grab three glasses. Fill one with ice water, one with room temperature water, and one with hot water (but make sure it isn't hot enough to burn you).

Hold the hot glass in one hand and the cold glass in the other. Your palms should be fully touching the glasses.

After one minute, put the glasses down and pick up the room temperature glass with both hands, touching the glass with your palms. Does the glass feel the same temperature to both hands?

You probably noticed that the third glass feels cooler to the hand that was holding the hot glass and warmer to the hand that was holding the cold glass. This is because your skin does not sense the exact temperature of an object. Instead, it senses the difference in temperature between a new object and an old object.

CARE AND FEEDING: YOUR DIGESTIVE SYSTEM

Your digestive system is like a long, twisting tube that runs from one end of your body to the other. It breaks down the food you eat so your body gets the nutrients it needs to work well and stay healthy. Your digestive system also helps your body get rid of waste it doesn't need, much of which leaves your body as poop (otherwise known as stool).

TOP 5 FUN FACTS

1. Your mouth makes up to 3 pints of saliva every single day, which is almost enough to fill a half-gallon container of milk!

2. It takes 7 seconds for the food you swallow to travel down your esophagus to your stomach.

3. The acid in your stomach, called *hydrochloric acid*, is also found in some industrial cleaners.

4. If you could stretch out your small intestine and lay it flat on the ground, it would cover an area the size of a tennis court.

5. Your large intestine contains 400 different types of tiny living things called *bacteria*, which help with digesting your food.

Digestion begins in the **MOUTH**, where your teeth and saliva break down large pieces of food.

The **SALIVARY GLANDS** produce saliva, a liquid that helps break down food when it enters your mouth.

The **ESOPHAGUS** carries food from the mouth to the stomach.

The **STOMACH** uses hydrochloric acid to break down food. After 3 to 4 hours, the food moves into the small intestine.

The **LIVER** and **GALL BLADDER** make and store a greenish-brown liquid called *bile*. Bile helps break down fat in the small intestines.

As food goes through the **SMALL INTESTINE**, the body takes in the nutrients and minerals it needs.

The **LARGE INTESTINE** absorbs water and turns the remaining food into poop.

Poop goes through the **RECTUM** and out the **ANUS** to exit the body.

ACTIVITY

Find and circle the words in the grid below:

```
Q  I  N  T  E  S  T  I  N  E
W  E  P  L  M  V  L  A  S  D
E  S  M  N  P  L  I  M  O  E
B  O  V  B  I  N  V  W  E  V
N  P  A  N  C  R  E  A  S  M
M  H  Z  I  N  U  R  C  O  F
Z  A  N  J  Y  N  C  W  L  M
X  G  C  I  K  L  D  E  T  Y
C  U  V  N  W  M  O  U  T  H
A  S  T  O  M  A  C  H  N  L
```

WORD BANK

mouth

esophagus

stomach

intestine

liver

pancreas

➡ Try This at Home

To learn how the stomach breaks down food, get a quart-size zip-top plastic bag, two crackers, and a quarter cup of soda.

Put the crackers into the plastic bag. Close the top, then use your hands to smash the crackers into small bits.

Now open the bag and pour in the soda. Close the top, then squish the bag to break the crackers down even more.

This shows how your stomach breaks food down both physically—by mashing it—and chemically—using hydrochloric acid.

FEEL THE BEAT:
YOUR HEART AND CIRCULATION

Your circulatory system is made up of your heart and blood vessels. This hardworking system pumps blood around your body at all hours of the day and night. As your heart pumps blood to all the parts of your body, your cells get the oxygen they need to work. And as your blood returns to your heart, it carries waste from the cells to organs called *kidneys*. Kidneys remove the waste so it can leave your body as pee (otherwise known as urine). This constant circulation of blood throughout your body keeps you alive.

TOP 5 FUN FACTS

1. Your heart is just a bit larger than your fist.

2. If you laid all your blood vessels end to end, they would measure 60,000 miles and wrap around the earth more than two times.

3. Your heart beats about 35 million times per year and about 3 billion times during your life.

4. It takes 16 seconds for blood to go from your heart to your toes and back.

5. Blood is never blue, even if it looks that way from the outside. Your veins carry blood without much oxygen. This blood is dark red but looks blue under your skin.

➡ Try This at Home

Find your pulse by putting two fingers from one hand on the inside wrist of your other arm. Slide your fingers across your wrist until they are close to the thumb side of the wrist just below your palm. When you feel your pulse, count the number of beats in one minute and write it down. Next, jog in place or do jumping jacks for 60 seconds. Find your pulse again and count the number of beats in one minute. How are these numbers different?

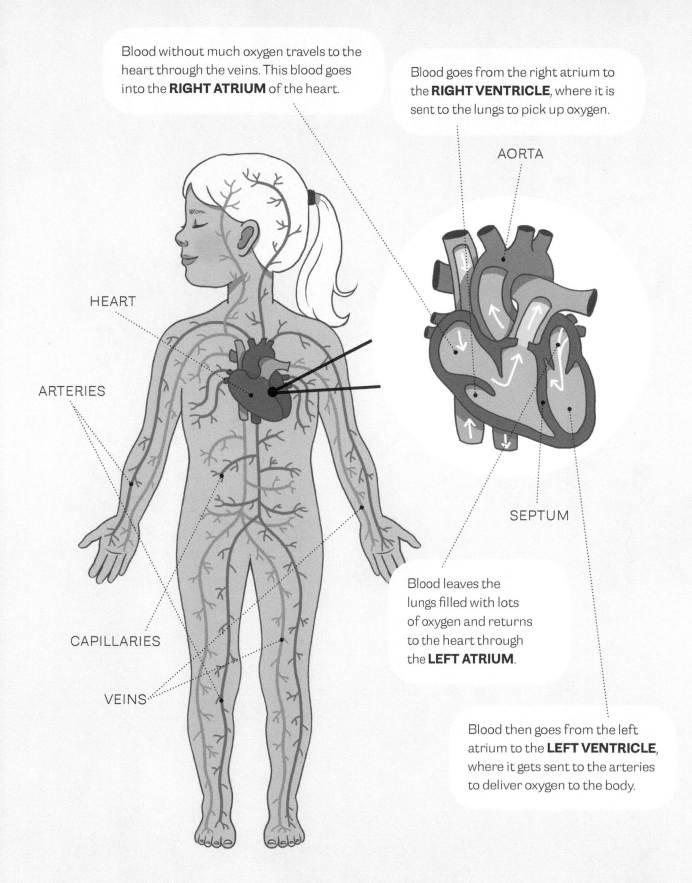

Blood without much oxygen travels to the heart through the veins. This blood goes into the **RIGHT ATRIUM** of the heart.

Blood goes from the right atrium to the **RIGHT VENTRICLE**, where it is sent to the lungs to pick up oxygen.

AORTA

HEART

ARTERIES

CAPILLARIES

VEINS

SEPTUM

Blood leaves the lungs filled with lots of oxygen and returns to the heart through the **LEFT ATRIUM**.

Blood then goes from the left atrium to the **LEFT VENTRICLE**, where it gets sent to the arteries to deliver oxygen to the body.

ACTIVITY

Blood travels around your body in small tubes called arteries, which carry blood *away* from the heart, and veins, which carry blood *toward* the heart.

Most **arteries** carry bright red blood with lots of oxygen. In this picture, the parts of the circulatory system that carry oxygen-rich blood are labeled with the number 1. Color them <u>red</u>.

Veins carry dark red blood without much oxygen. In this picture, the parts of the circulatory system that carry oxygen-poor blood are labeled with the number 2. Color them <u>blue</u>.

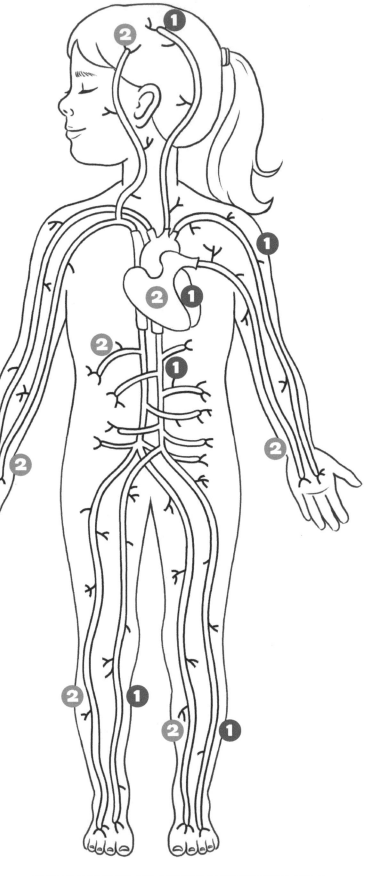

DEEP BREATHS: YOUR LUNGS AND RESPIRATION

In order to stay alive, your body is always taking in oxygen. That is why your lungs are so important. Your lungs take oxygen from the air and deliver it to the blood to be transported around your body. Your lungs also remove carbon dioxide from the blood for you to breathe back out.

TOP 5 FUN FACTS

1. You take 15 to 30 breaths per minute, or 21,000 to 42,000 breaths per day.

2. It is impossible for you to breathe and swallow at the same time.

3. Your left lung is 10 percent smaller than your right lung in order to make room for your heart.

4. After one minute without oxygen, brain cells begin to die.

5. There are over 300 million tiny blood vessels called *capillaries* in your lungs. If you stretched them all out, they would reach across the United States.

NASAL CAVITY

Air goes in the nose or mouth, then travels down the **TRACHEA** to get to the lungs.

The **LUNGS** work closely with the heart to deliver oxygen to the body and take out carbon dioxide.

RIGHT LUNG

LEFT LUNG

BRONCHIAL TUBES

The **DIAPHRAGM** is a large muscle just below the lungs that gets bigger and smaller to help the lungs take air in and out.

Inside the lungs, air goes through the **BRONCHIAL TUBES**, which split into smaller tubes called **BRONCHIOLES**. At the end of the bronchioles are tiny air sacs called **ALVEOLI**.

ALVEOLI

BRONCHIOLES

ACTIVITY

Help the oxygen (O_2) get to the alveoli in the lungs.

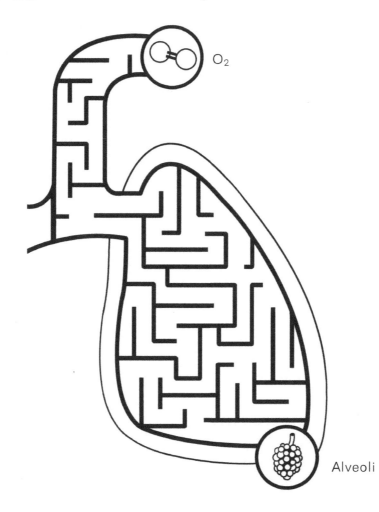

O_2

Alveoli

➡️ Try This at Home

Feel your lungs and diaphragm in action. Put one hand on your chest and the other on your belly, then take a big breath in. Feel your chest and belly get bigger as the air goes into your lungs. Now breathe out. Feel your chest and belly get smaller as the air goes out of your lungs.

Now breathe in as slowly as you can. Count the seconds it takes until you fill your lungs with air. Then breathe out as slowly as you can. Count the seconds it takes until you finish breathing out. This kind of deep breathing is great for helping you feel calmer when you are worried or upset.

STAY STRONG: YOUR IMMUNE SYSTEM

Your immune system is made up of cells, tissues, and organs that protect your body against infection and help you stay healthy. Your immune system finds harmful germs and sends white blood cells to get rid of those germs. This stops you from getting sick or helps you start feeling better.

TOP 5 FUN FACTS

1. Your body has about 35 billion white blood cells when you are healthy. It makes even more when you are sick.

2. Your body actually needs some bacteria to stay healthy. There are bacteria in your intestines, for example, that keep your immune system in tip-top shape.

3. You may not feel good when you have a fever, but having one helps your body get rid of germs.

4. Stress and not getting enough sleep can hurt your immune system, making you more likely to get sick.

5. Laughter may actually be the best medicine! Happy feelings help you have a healthy immune system.

➡ Try This at Home

Use water or lotion to dampen your hands, then sprinkle glitter on your palms and rub them together. Next, shake hands with a partner or place your palm on a piece of paper. Notice the trail of "germs" you leave behind? Now wash your hands with plain water. How well do the "germs" come off? Then wash your hands with soap and water. How well do the "germs" come off now? Washing with soap and water keeps germs from spreading.

TONSILS AND ADENOIDS trap germs that enter through the mouth and nose.

The **THYMUS** trains white blood cells to protect against infection.

The **SPLEEN** stores white blood cells and fights harmful bacteria.

LYMPH NODES remove harmful bacteria and viruses.

BONE MARROW makes white and red blood cells.

WHITE BLOOD CELLS find germs and remove them from the body.

The **SKIN** has special cells that warn the body about germs.

ACTIVITY

Draw a line from each part of the immune system to a place in the body where it is found.

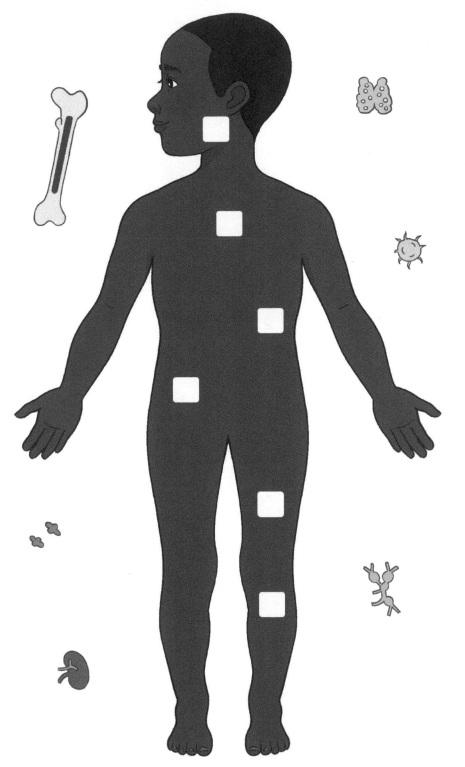

TAKING CARE OF YOUR BODY

You only get one body, so it is very important to take care of it! You can do this by eating healthy foods, including lots of fruits and vegetables. You should get enough sleep at night, so you wake up feeling rested. You should exercise to keep your bones and muscles strong. And you should do things that make you happy because your feelings have a big effect on your health too.

TOP 5 FUN FACTS

1. One of the most important things you can do to stay healthy is to eat real food. If something looks like it was made in a factory, it's usually better not to eat it. If it comes from a plant or tree, it's probably good for you.

2. Half of all children don't have enough of at least one important nutrient. Eating many different kinds of colorful fruits and vegetables is an important way to get the nutrients you need.

3. The fastest human on earth can run at speeds of nearly 28 miles per hour. If you could run at that rate without resting, it would take you a little less than 4 days to cross the United States.

4. Your body makes special germ-fighting proteins while you sleep. When you don't get enough rest, you are more likely to get sick.

5. For good health, kids need about 10 to 11 hours of sleep each night.

BENEFITS OF EXERCISE

Your brain gets more oxygen, making you smarter.

You feel happier.

Your muscles get bigger and stronger.

Your heart gets healthier.

Your bones get stronger and thicker.

ACTIVITY

Find and circle the words in the grid below.

R K O W E A T V E S
M S E P R D Z U H T
G T H V Y A H B L R
E X E R C I S E W O
A L A L S O F L I N
N Y L J C I M K E G
Q E T E F N O L T M
I S H I M O B I P C
D H Y D N E Y V G A
Z A X U C S L E E P

WORD BANK

healthy

exercise

live

strong

eat

sleep

➡ Try This at Home

Staying healthy is about having good eating, exercise, sleep, and emotional habits. Grab a piece of paper and a pencil, then write down one thing you will do to get plenty of exercise, one healthy food you will eat more of, one idea for getting plenty of sleep, and one thing you will do because it makes you happy. Post it somewhere you can see it often to remind yourself of what you plan to do.

RESOURCES

Books

Me and My Amazing Body by Joan Sweeney: A simple introduction to the human body that answers young children's basic questions. Ages 3 to 7.

Little Explorers: My Amazing Body by Ruth Martin: A lift-the-flaps book that allows children to find out what goes on under their skin. Ages 4 to 8.

My First Human Body Book by Patricia J. Wynne and Donald M. Silver: Includes ready-to-color illustrations of various systems in the human body. Ages 5 to 9.

The Magic School Bus Presents: The Human Body by Tom Jackson: A photographic nonfiction book based on *The Magic School Bus* series. Ages 6 to 10.

First Human Body Encyclopedia from DK: A great introduction to the inner workings of the human body. Ages 7 to 11.

Human Body! by DK: A visual encyclopedia featuring computer-generated 3-D imagery of the body. Ages 9 to 12.

Digital Resources

My Incredible Body (www.visiblebody.com/anatomy-and-physiology-apps/anatomy-for-kids): This app for your phone or tablet gives children the chance to play and learn by exploring inside immersive 3-D models. Ages 5 to 10.

How the Body Works (kidshealth.org/en/kids/htbw/): This website includes links to printable activities for each body system. Ages 6 to 10.

Human Biology (www.education.com/resources/human+biology/): This website includes images, video, and additional information about each of the major body systems. Ages 6 to 10.

Human Body for Kids (www.sciencekids.co.nz/humanbody.html): This website features games, experiments, quizzes, images, and projects for learning about the human body. Ages 7 to 11.

Innerbody
(www.innerbody.com/htm/body.html):
This website includes details about the main body systems and allows children to explore both 2-D and 3-D models of the body. Ages 8 to 12.

Human Anatomy Atlas
(www.visiblebody.com/anatomy-and
-physiology-apps/human-anatomy-atlas):
This app for your phone or tablet gives children the opportunity to interact with complete 3-D anatomy models. Ages 10 and up.

Games and Models

Magnetic Human Body Anatomy Play Set from Melissa & Doug: Includes magnetic pieces for building different body systems. Ages 3 to 6.

What's Inside Me Anatomy Apron from Yoovi: A wearable apron with removeable organs made from fabric. Ages 4 to 8.

Magnetic Human Body from Learning Resources: Reversible magnetic pieces that children can assemble into a 3-foot tall body showing the skeleton on one side and the muscles and organs on the other. Ages 5 to 9.

Squishy Human Body from SmartLab Toys: 3-D model of the human body with removable body parts and companion book showing how a slice of pizza moves through the digestive system. Ages 6 to 10.

Fascinating Facts Human Body Game from Lakeshore: Explore the human body from the inside out with a 10.5-inch model and quiz cards. Ages 7 to 11.

Anatomy Models Bundle Set from Learning Resources: Includes small plastic models of the body, brain, heart, and skeleton for children to assemble. Ages 8 and up.

INDEX

ABOUT THE AUTHOR

KATIE STOKES received her B.A. in human biology; her M.Ed. in policy, organization, and leadership studies; and her Ph.D. in child development from Stanford University. In addition, she has more than 20 years of experience working with children from preschool through high school.

Katie founded *Gift of Curiosity* to share hands-on, developmentally appropriate learning activities for children with parents, teachers, and caregivers all over the world. Her most important job, however, is partnering with her husband to raise two curious children whom she educates at home. See more of Katie's work at www.GiftOfCuriosity.com.

CPSIA information can be obtained
at www.ICGtesting.com
Printed in the USA
JSHW030725240920
8145JS00014B/48

9 781641 522632